Learn Braille
Uncontracted (Grade 1) & Contracted (Grade 2)

R. J. Clarke

Copyright © 2016 **R. J. Clarke**

All rights reserved.

ISBN-13: 978-1539368137
ISBN-10: 1539368130

Contents

Introduction to uncontracted braille 1
    The Braille Cell 2
    Letters 3
    Punctuation 5
    Numbers 32
    Typeforms 52
    Simple Arrows 58
    Simple Shapes 59
    UEB Music 61
    Foreign Letters 62
Introduction to contracted braille 66
    Grade 1 Indicators 67
    Alphabetic Wordsigns 68
    Final-letter Groupsigns 70
    Initial-letter Contractions 72
    Strong Wordsigns 77
    Strong Groupsigns 78
    Strong Contractions 79
    Lower Groupsigns 80
    Lower Wordsigns 82
    Shortforms 83
Preferences 86
Braille Courses 87
Bibliography 88

Introduction to Uncontracted (Grade 1) Braille

In 1821, a blind French boy named Louis Braille (1809-1852) enabled blind and visually impaired people to read and write through the use of touch.

Braille has evolved a lot since then and the standard braille used in all of the major English-speaking countries is called UEB (Unified English Braille). This was developed by the *International Council on English Braille* and different countries have adopted this standard at different times:

- Australia (2005)
- New Zealand (2005)
- Canada (2010)
- United Kingdom (2011)
- United States (2012)

UEB consists of uncontracted and contracted braille, which were previously known as grade 1 and grade 2 braille respectively. Uncontracted braille is the simplest to learn because a single letter, number or punctuation is represented by a single braille cell.

Learning uncontracted braille will enable someone to read and write, which could be useful for creating labels for household items as well playing a game of cards or Scrabble.

The Braille Cell

A braille cell consists of six dot positions that are arranged in two vertical columns and three horizontal rows. The presence or absence of dots gives rise to 64 combinations to represent letters, punctuation and numbers.

By convention, the position of the dots in a braille cell are numbered 1-3 from the top left corner down. Then 4-6 from the top right hand corner down. Numbering is only used to clarify the dot positions of a character and it is not actually used for reading or writing braille.

1 ● ● 4
2 ● ● 5
3 ● ● 6

Throughout this book, there will be two types of dots:

● a raised dot position

○ an absent dot position

Letters

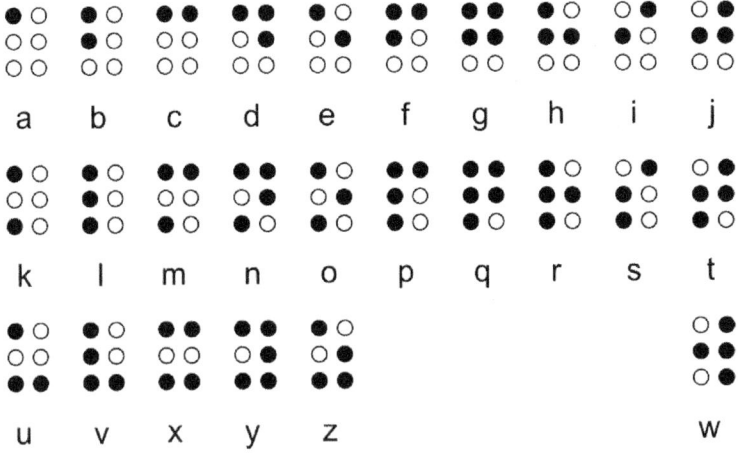

At first glance, the braille alphabet may seem difficult to remember but if you notice carefully:

- The letters from a–j all have the dots 3 and 6 absent.
- The letters k–t are the same as a–j but with the addition of dot 3.
- The letters u–z (except w) are the same as a–j but with the addition of dots 3 and 6.

The reason why the letter w does not follow any pattern is because braille was developed in France. There is no letter w in the French language so the braille letter for w had to be added at a later date.

Capital Letters

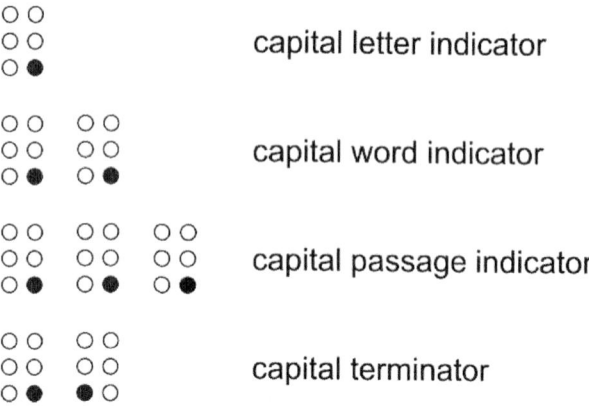

A capital letter is used for proper nouns (the name of a person, place or organization) as well as the first letter of a word that begins a sentence or a quoted sentence. Furthermore, the main words in titles are in capitals such as an animated TV show called - Shaun the Sheep

Please note that small capitals such as those found in Roman Numerals and newspaper headlines should be brailled as ordinary capital letters.

Punctuation

Punctuation is an essential part of braille because it helps people to understand sentences.

The different types of punctuation in this book are explained so that you will be able to read and write braille effectively.

Some punctuation rules vary depending on which country you live in. Fortunately, I have provided information so that you will know the difference between British English and American English and use the one that applies to you.

Apostrophe

⠀' apostrophe

An apostrophe is used to represent a missing letter or letters in a contraction e.g. do not = don't

d o n ' t

An apostrophe can also be used to show possession e.g. the girl's necklace. This means that one girl has a necklace. However, if there was no apostrophe i.e. the girls necklace, this would mean that more than one girl would be sharing one necklace.

t h e   g i r l ' s   n e c k l a c e

Ampersand

⠀⠨⠯ & ampersand

An Ampersand is a punctuation symbol that means and. Ampersands are sometimes used in company names as well as common expressions e.g. B&B (Bed and Breakfast)

⠠⠃ ⠯ ⠠⠃
B & B

⠠⠎⠍⠊⠞⠓ ⠯ ⠠⠎⠕⠝⠎
Smith   &   Sons

Asterisk

⠀⠀* asterisk

An asterisk can be used to represent an omitted letter such as those in swear words.

s * * *

An asterisk can also be used to indicate a footnote, which will provide further details at the bottom of the page. Symbol footnotes such as an asterisk are usually used after titles, headings and author names. However, they can also be used in short texts such as advertisements.

free pen *

* limited   stock

Please note that lettered footnotes are usually used in an annex, appendix, figure or table. Whilst, numbered footnotes are usually used in the main text of a long document.

Brackets – Round and Square

(opening round bracket

) closing round bracket

[opening square bracket

] closing square bracket

Round brackets are also known as parenthesis and they are used to add extra information. They can also be used to show that something could be plural e.g. guest(s)

g u e s t (s)

Square brackets are used to clarify information. They can also be used to indicate a spelling mistake in a quotation e.g. misteak [sic]

m i s t e a k   [s i c]

9

Brackets – Curly and Angle

{ opening curly bracket

} closing curly bracket

< opening angle bracket

> closing angle bracket

Curly brackets are also known as braces and they do very occasionally appear in normal writing. However, they are mainly used in mathematics, science and computing.

{ v a r i a b l e }

Angle brackets are also known as chevrons and they are commonly used in mathematics to represent the comparison signs: less than (<) and greater than (>). Angle brackets are sometimes used to enclose email and website addresses. They are also used in computer programming languages such as HTML (Hyper Text Markup Language).

< h t m l >

Brackets – Large

⠠⠣ (opening large round bracket

⠠⠜) closing large round bracket

A large bracket spans multiple lines on printed text. It is commonly used in mathematics to show a matrix or vector, but these large brackets can be found in ordinary text to group something together. Here is an example:

cat

dog

bird

animals

In printed text, the text following a large bracket is usually centered vertically. However, in braille, this text is placed on the top line. Furthermore, the braille large bracket symbol is aligned vertically on each line and a blank line usually exists before and after the use of large brackets to make their usage clearer.

Please note that the second braille cell of a large bracket can be replaced with a square or curly bracket.

Bullet Point

⠤ • bullet point

A bullet point is sometimes used in lists when the order is not important. They must be introduced by a colon and each sentence must make sense when following it. Furthermore, each sentence in a bullet point must have a consistent style i.e. if you choose to start each sentence with a capital and end them with a period, you should do the same for the rest.

Useful products:
· talking clock
· tactile dots
· white cane

Please note that there needs to be a blank space on each side of a bullet point.

Comma

, comma

Commas are useful for indicating a brief pause, listing a series of three or more things and separating words so that the meaning of a sentence is not misunderstood. Commas are also used when introducing quotations e.g. she said, "something"

it is summer,
however, it is cold
eat, sleep and read
when she spoke, her
mind was elsewhere

Daggers

⠀⠻⠶ † dagger

⠀⠻⠶ ‡ double dagger

A dagger is used to indicate a second footnote, whilst a double dagger is used to indicate a third footnote.

The order in which symbol footnotes are used is usually:

*   Asterisk
†   Dagger
‡   Double Dagger
§   Section mark

Another use for the dagger is to indicate the extinction of a species or the death of a person. The dagger symbol is used either before or after the name of a species or person.

Charlie †

Dashes

— em dash

– en dash

The em dash is the same length as the letter m. It can have a space or no space either side and it is used to create pauses or extensions to sentences. The em dash can also be used instead of commas, colons and brackets

my brothers —

Kirk, Matt and

Kris — are kind

The en dash is the same length as the letter n. It has no space either side and it is often used for a range of numbers e.g. World War II lasted from 1939-1945. The en dash can also be used for linking pairs of related words before a noun e.g. pupil-teacher ratio

pupil-teacher ratio

Ditto

 " ditto

Ditto is a symbol that means the same again. It is used in lists to represent that the above word is repeated. The ditto symbol is placed in the middle (or near the middle) of each repeated word.

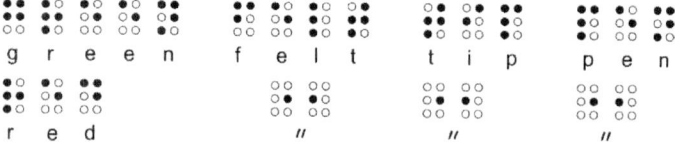

Please note that a ditto mark may look similar to a double quotation mark in printed text, but they have different braille symbols.

Ellipsis

... ellipsis

An ellipsis consists of three periods (full stops) and is used to represent a missing word, phrase or sentence. This use is often found when shortening long quotations. The ellipsis can also be used to express hesitation, suspense or an unfinished thought that trails into silence.

u h . . .   o k

t h e   d o o r   o p e n e d . . .

w h a t   t h e . . .

Exclamation Point

⠀⠖ ! exclamation point

An exclamation point is known as an exclamation mark in British English and it is used at the end of a sentence, which expresses strong emotion such as shouting, enthusiasm or surprise.

s t o p !

we cannot wait !

it is a miracle !

Gender Symbols

♀ female sign

♂ male sign

Gender symbols are used to represent the sex of a person, plant or animal. An easy way to remember the second braille cell for the female and male signs is to think about the second chromosome, which is x for females and y for males.

♀ womens toilet

♂ mens toilet

Hashtag

⠼ # hashtag

A hashtag can be used as a number sign e.g. #1 means number one. A hashtag can also be used as a pound sign e.g. 5# means that something weighs five pounds. Finally, a hashtag can be used on social media networks (e.g. Facebook and Twitter) to mark a keyword so that it is easier to find content on a particular topic

the television

series #breaking bad

is amazing

Hyphen

⠀⠤ - hyphen

A hyphen is shorter than a dash and it can be used between compound words to clarify their meaning. For example, a man eating shark has a totally different meaning to a deadly man-eating shark.

```
m a n - e a t i n g   s h a r k
```

A hyphen is also used to split words that do not fit on the end of a line and they can occur in some prefixes e.g. co-operate

```
c o - o p e r a t e
```

Intellectual Property Symbols

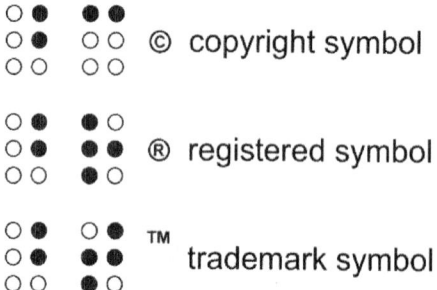

Intellectual property symbols may appear superscripted in printed text but in braille they do not.

```
c o p y r i g h t   ©

r e g i s t e r e d   ®

t r a d e m a r k   ™
```

Period (full stop)

⠨ . period (full stop)

A period is known as a full stop in British English and it is used at the end of a sentence. A period may also be used in an acronym e.g. F.A.Q. (Frequently Asked Questions) or an abbreviation e.g. dept. (department)

F . A . Q .

d e p t .

Please note that a person's title will have a period afterwards in American English but not in British English. An example of a person's title is Mrs.

Furthermore, periods stay on the outside of quotation marks in American English, but go on the inside in British English.

Question Mark

? question mark

A question mark is always used at the end of a sentence if there is a direct question to someone. However, a sentence with a rhetorical question can end in either a question mark, exclamation mark or period, depending on the context.

who said that?

Quotation Marks – Double and Single

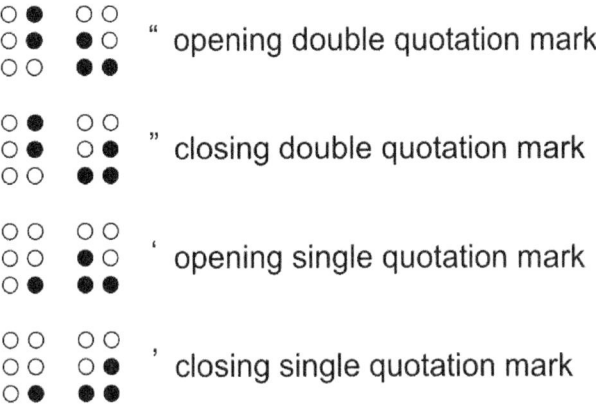

In American English, double quotation marks are used to indicate the start and end of spoken words, whilst single quotation marks are used inside double quotation marks when there is a quote or title inside a quote. Double and single quotation marks are used the other way around in British English.

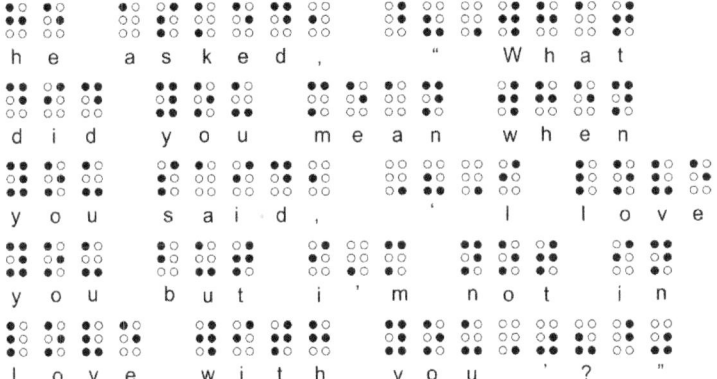

Quotation Mark - Guillemets

« opening guillemet

» closing guillemet

Guillemets are also known as angle quotation marks and they are used in many foreign countries to indicate speech. In most foreign countries, there is no space after an opening guillemet and no space before a closing guillemet. However, France is an exception. Also, some countries such as Germany use the opening and closing guillemet symbols the other way around.

« most countries »

« French »

» German «

Lastly, guillemets can be used to represent fast forward and rewind symbols.

press « to rewind

Quotation Mark – Nonspecific

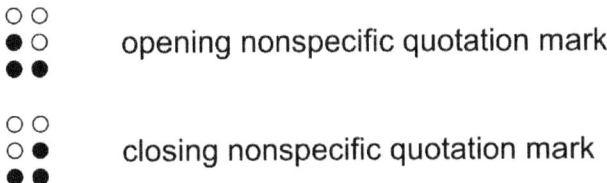

opening nonspecific quotation mark

closing nonspecific quotation mark

Nonspecific quotation marks are very common. They are used to represent the main quotation mark that is used throughout a document. Nonspecific quotation marks save a lot of space because they only occupy one braille cell, whilst a single or double quotation mark occupies two braille cells.

Marilyn Monroe said, "Good things fall apart so that better things can fall together."

Semicolon and Colon

⠰ ; semicolon

⠒ : colon

A semicolon is used to join two separate sentences that have closely related content. A semicolon is also used when listing something that has commas.

i have visited

London, England;

Paris, France; and

Rome, Italy

A colon is used to join two separate sentences when the second sentence contains an explanation or reason. A colon can also be used for introducing a list of items e.g. this is what I want: nuts, pears and kiwi

this is what i want:

nuts, pears and kiwi

Slashes

⠀⠸⠀⠘⠀ \ backward slash

⠀⠸⠀⠐⠀ / forward slash

A backward slash is rarely used but an example of its use would be in the filenames on computers running a Windows operating system.

```
C : \ p r o g r a m s
```

A forward slash is also known as a solidus and it is used in website addresses, fractions and to represent a choice between two or more words.

```
h e / s h e
```

Please note that a forward slash can be used in dates.

In American English, dates are written:
month / day / year

In British English, dates are written:
day / month / year

29

Underscore

⠨ _ underscore

The underscore is a low horizontal line and it is sometimes used in filenames, email addresses and to indicate a blank space in puzzles and forms.

p u _ _ l e s

s u r n a m e _

Please note that the underscore length is not represented in braille.

@ Symbol

○● ●○
○○ ○○   @ symbol
○○ ○○

The @ symbol simply means the word at. The @ symbol is commonly used in commercial invoices (e.g. 20 bags @ $5 each) as well as in email addresses.

n a m e @ g m a i l . c o m

Numbers

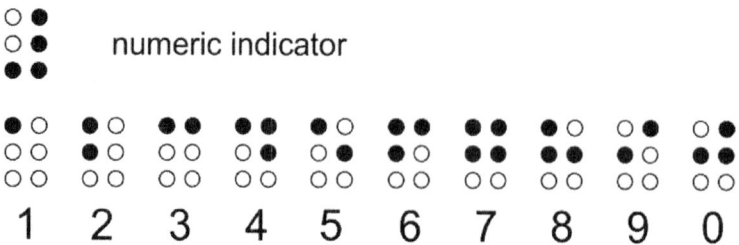

The numbers 1-9 share the same braille cells as the letters from a-i whilst the number 0 has the same braille cell as the letter j.

To prevent the numbers from being misread as a letter, it is important to use a numeric indicator to set the numeric mode.

The numeric indicator is always used before a number or set of numbers.

5

7 9

1 0 8

Numbers with Letters

grade 1 indicator

A grade 1 indicator is required if a number is followed by a lowercase letter from a-j. A grade 1 indicator is not used if a number is followed by a capital letter or a letter from k-z.

7 2   a

2 B

6 0 m

A grade 1 indicator is required if a number is followed by either a comma or period and then a lowercase letter from a-j.

d o c u m e n t   2 .   h t m l

Ordinal numbers such as 1st, 2nd, 3rd and 4th are sometimes printed with a space between the number and letter. However, when they are brailled, there is no space and the letters are not superscripted either.

1 s t

Numbers with Punctuation

A comma is often used in large numbers to make them easier to read.

⠼⠁⠂⠚⠚⠚⠂⠚⠚⠚
1 , 0 0 0 , 0 0 0

A period can be used in a number to indicate a decimal point.

section   1.2

Please note that a numeric indicator will come after a period if it is not used as a decimal point.

I live at no. 79

The only punctuation and symbols allowed in numeric mode are: numbers, periods, commas, simple fraction lines and line continuation indicators. Anything else will terminate the numeric mode.

1 9 1 4 - 1 9 1 8

Numbers with Spaces

⠀⠐⠀ numeric space

An ordinary space will terminate the numeric mode. Therefore, it is important to use the braille symbol for a numeric space in long numbers that contain at least one space. For example, a credit card number is 16 digits long and is broken into 4 segments.

```
1 2 3 4  5 6 7 8  9 0 1 2  3 4 5 6
```

Please note that an ordinary space is used to separate numbers if they are intended to be treated as separate numbers.

the winning lottery

numbers are: 1 3   2 1

3 0   3 9   5 1   5 9

Numbers Split Between Lines

⠀⠠ line continuation indicator

Line continuation indicators are usually only used for extremely long numbers that cannot fit on to a single line. An example would be Pi to 50 places:

3 . 1 4 1 5 9 2 6 5 3 5 8 9 7 9 3
2 3 8 4 6 2 6 4 3 3 8 3 2 7 9 5 0 2
8 8 4 1 9 7 1 6 9 3 9 9 3 7 5 1 0

Please note that a line continuation indicator is used at the end of a line and it does not terminate the numeric mode. Also, it has the same braille cell as a numeric indicator and it is preferable if a line continuation indicator is used in a logical place such as after a comma or a numeric space.

Basic Mathematics

○ ○ ○ ○
○ ● ● ●   + addition sign
○ ○ ● ○

○ ○ ○ ○
○ ● ○ ○   - minus sign
○ ○ ● ●

○ ○ ○ ○
○ ● ● ○   x multiplication sign
○ ○ ● ●

○ ○ ○ ●
○ ● ○ ○   ÷ division sign
○ ○ ● ○

○ ○ ○ ○
○ ● ● ●   = equals sign
○ ○ ● ●

In braille, there is usually no space between the operation signs: plus, minus, multiplication and division. However, a space is usually used for the comparison signs: greater than, less than and equal to.

  4   x   7   =   2 8

Please note that the letter x is never used to represent the multiplication sign.

37

Caret

⠀⠈⠀ ⠀⠀ ^ caret

A caret is a proofreading symbol that is placed before newly inserted words. A caret can also be used as an upward arrow as well as in mathematics to show an exponential function. For example: 7^10 would be said as, "seven to the power of ten"

7^10 = 7 x 7 x 7 x 7 x 7 x 7 x 7 x 7 x 7 x 7

⠀⠀⠀⠀⠀⠀⠀⠀⠀⠀⠀⠀⠀
7   ^   1 0

Please note that a different braille symbol is used to represent a caret above a character (see page 64)

Currency

⠨⠉ ¢ Cent

⠨⠙ $ Dollar

⠨⠑ € Euro

⠨⠇ £ Pound

⠨⠽ ¥ Yen

Any currency can be created by adding either letters or transcriber-defined symbols (see page 49)

5 0 ¢

$ 2 5

€ 9 . 9 9

£ 1 m   (m is short for million)

¥ 1 0 , 0 0 0

Degrees

⠘⠚ degree

The degree symbol is used in angles, temperatures and map coordinates measured in decimal degrees.

a circle is 360°

20°C = 68°F

lat: 52.420105°

long: 1.722304°

Feet and Inches

⠄ ' feet

⠄⠄ " inches

The feet symbol is also known as a prime symbol and there is 3 feet in 1 yard.

  5 '   5 "   t a l l

The inches symbol is also known as a double prime symbol and there is 12 inches in 1 foot.

  6 "   l o n g

The symbols for feet and inches can also be used with a degree symbol to form map coordinates measured in degrees, minutes and seconds.

5 2 ° 2 5 ' 1 2 . 3 8 " N

1 ° 4 3 ' 2 0 . 2 9 5 " E

An apostrophe can be used instead of a feet symbol.

Fractions – Simple and Linear

⠠⠀ simple numeric fraction line
⠀⠀
⠂⠀

⠐⠀ ⠐⠀   linear fraction line
⠐⠀ ⠀⠀
⠐⠀ ⠂⠀

A simple numeric fraction has a line between a number that is above another number. These types of fractions can only be composed of numbers that can contain decimal points, commas and numeric spaces. Also, the simple numeric fraction line does not terminate the numeric mode. However, another numeric indicator is used if there is a number before an unspaced fraction.

$\frac{1}{2}$ ⠼⠁⠌⠼⠃
      1   2

3 ¼   ⠼⠉⠼⠁⠌⠼⠙
      3 1 4

A linear fraction has a forward slash between two numbers e.g. 2/3. The forward slash does terminate the numeric mode, so it is necessary to add another numeric indicator.

2 / 3   ⠼⠃⠸⠌⠼⠉
      2   3

Fractions - General

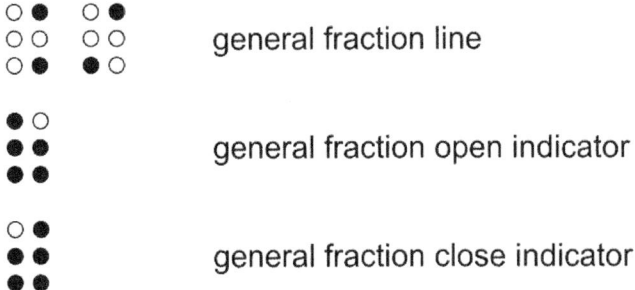

general fraction line

general fraction open indicator

general fraction close indicator

A general fraction has a horizontal line between a numerator and denominator. These must contain at least one letter or symbol that is not allowed in a simple numeric fraction.

$\frac{x}{y}$ ⠀ x ⠀ y

$\frac{24cm}{6cm}$ ⠀ 2 4 c m ⠀ 6 c m

$\frac{?}{8}$ ⠀ ? ⠀ 8

$\frac{17-2}{5}$ ⠀ 1 7 - 2 ⠀ 5

$\frac{\$20}{4}$ ⠀ $ 2 0 ⠀ 4

Please note that this type of fraction is enclosed with general fraction open and close indicators.

Percentages

⠸⠴ % percent

The percent sign is used to indicate a fraction out of 100. The usage of this sign varies between different grammar and style guides. The differences include whether or not to use a space before the sign, and the circumstances of when to use the word percent instead of the sign.

If you are transcribing braille, follow the same style found in printed text.

    1 0 %

    1 0   %

    1 0   p e r c e n t

Section and Paragraphs

¶ paragraph sign

§ section sign

Paragraph (also called pilcrow) and section signs are typically found in long legal documents where page numbers do not exist. They are used when citing a particular paragraph or section as a reference.

¶ 5

§ 4

Two section signs are used when there is a range of sections.

§ § 1 - 3

A good way of learning these braille signs is to remember that the second braille symbol is the first letter of the word i.e. p = paragraph and s = section

Square Roots

⠠⠶ open root

⠠⠴ close root

Square roots are used in mathematics. The square root of a number is equal to a number that can be multiplied by itself. For example, the square root of 25 equals 5 because 5 squared (5 x 5) equals 25.

$\sqrt{25} = 5$

Subscript and Superscript

⠰ subscript indicator

⠘ superscript indicator

Subscript means that a letter, number or symbol has had its font size reduced and is lowered relative to the text it is adjacent to. Subscripts are typically used in chemical formulas e.g. the chemical compound for water is H_2O

H   2   O

Superscript means that a letter, number or symbol has had its font size reduced and is raised relative to the text it is adjacent to. Superscripts are typically used in footnotes and in mathematics e.g. x^2

x   2

Tilde

⠠⠔ ~ tilde

Tilde is also known as a swung dash and it means approximately.

dinner will be ready in ~ 15 minutes

A tilde can also be used in mathematics e.g. x ~ y
This means that x is equivalent to y

x ~ y

Please note that another braille symbol is used when using a tilde above a character (see page 64)

Transcriber-Defined Symbols

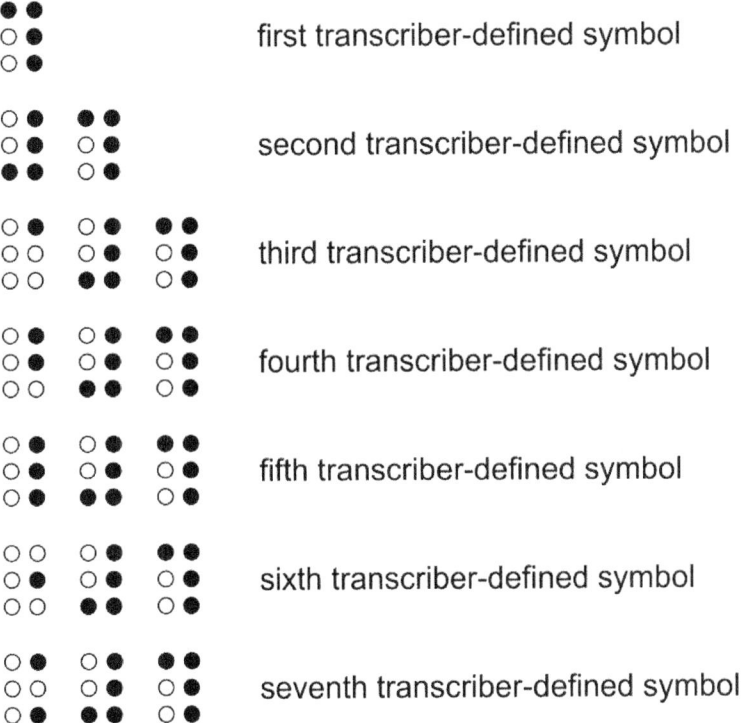

A transcriber-defined symbol can be used for any symbol that is not known in braille. For example, a per mille (parts per thousand) symbol could be listed on a Symbols Page as the first transcriber-defined symbol.

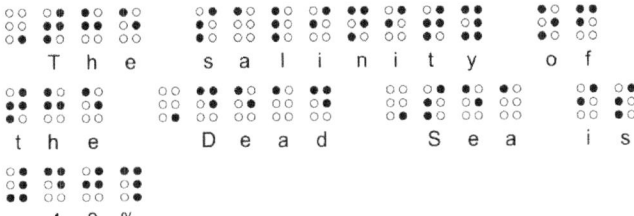

Special Symbols Page

A Special Symbols Page is often found after the title page of a braille book. Its purpose is to inform the braille reader of any symbols that they will not know about because their braille cells have been defined by the transcriber.

The page should be titled – Special Symbols. Then, the symbols should be in a list in the order of when they are first encountered. Next to each symbol, the name or meaning should be brailled.

Transcriber's Note Indicators

⠀⠂　⠀⠂　⠐⠀　　opening transcriber's note indicator

⠀⠂　⠀⠂　⠀⠂　　closing transcriber's note indicator

Transcriber note indicators occur in the main text and they are used by a transcriber to provide an explanation of how they decided to transcribe printed text into braille. Here is an example:

```
These tables
are side by side in
print
```

Please note that there is no space after an opening transcriber's note indicator and there is no space before a closing transcriber's note indicator.

Typeforms

A typeform is also known as a font attribute and the four main types are bold, italics, script and underline.

Typeforms have two braille cells. The first braille cell determines which typeform is used, whilst the second braille cell controls the extent of its use i.e. the next symbol, word or passage.

If a word has multiple typeforms such as being bold and underlined (e.g. **word**), it is necessary to do something called nesting. This means that the indicators should be closed in the reverse order. To clarify this, here is an example of the order for a bold and underlined word:

1) Bold word indicator
2) Underline word indicator
3) A word
4) Underline terminator
5) Bold terminator

Sometimes it is necessary to use a new typeform and this can be achieved by using a transcriber-defined typeform. An example of this, would be to show a word with a strikethrough because it indicates a mistake or change of thought.

Bold

⠀⠸⠀⠈⠀ bold symbol indicator

⠀⠸⠀⠘⠀ bold word indicator

⠀⠸⠀⠸⠀ bold passage indicator

⠀⠸⠀⠐⠀ bold terminator

Bold is a font attribute that makes text thicker. Titles, headings and subheadings are often made bold in printed text, but it is not the case with braille because the location of the text is usually enough to indicate its purpose. Bold text should only be transcribed in braille if it is necessary to show emphasis or distinction.

click on the **next level** button

Italics

⠀⠨⠀⠀⠀⠀ italic symbol indicator

⠀⠨⠀⠀⠀⠀ italic word indicator

⠀⠨⠀⠀⠆⠆ italic passage indicator

⠀⠨⠀⠀⠀⠄ italic terminator

Italics is a font attribute that provides emphasis to text by causing it to slant to the right. It occurs in a sentence that refers to the title of books, movies, music etc. Foreign words and scientific names are often in italics and so is the sound of reproduced words such as *grrr*.

⠀⠨⠀⠀⠐⠆⠀⠀⠗⠀⠀⠐⠗⠀⠀⠨⠗
   g   r   r   r

Sometimes a word is in italics for emphasis, which can change the meaning significantly. For example:

I didn't tell her (someone else did)
I *didn't* tell her (I definitely did not)
I didn't *tell* her (I implied it instead)
I didn't tell *her* (I told someone else)

54

Script

⠂⠀⠀⠄		script symbol indicator
⠂⠀⠀⠄		script word indicator
⠂⠀⠀⠆⠆		script passage indicator
⠂⠀⠀⠠		script terminator

Script is a font attribute that is normally used to represent handwritten text. It should only be used if its use has a purpose beyond being ornamental.

the words *dear*

diary was written

in her diary

Underline

⠨⠱ underlined symbol indicator

⠨⠜ underlined word indicator

⠨⠐⠜ underlined passage indicator

⠨⠤ underlined terminator

An underline is a horizontal line that is below a letter, punctuation or number e.g. <u>underline</u>. It is common for titles and hyperlinks to be underlined in printed text but the underline does not appear in braille because it would only serve an ornamental purpose. However, an underline can be used in braille to distinguish it from other text as long as it is important for its understanding. For example, an embedded link may be underlined because otherwise its existence would not be known.

he sells <u>seven</u> <u>more</u>
<u>books</u> online

Transcriber-Defined Typeforms

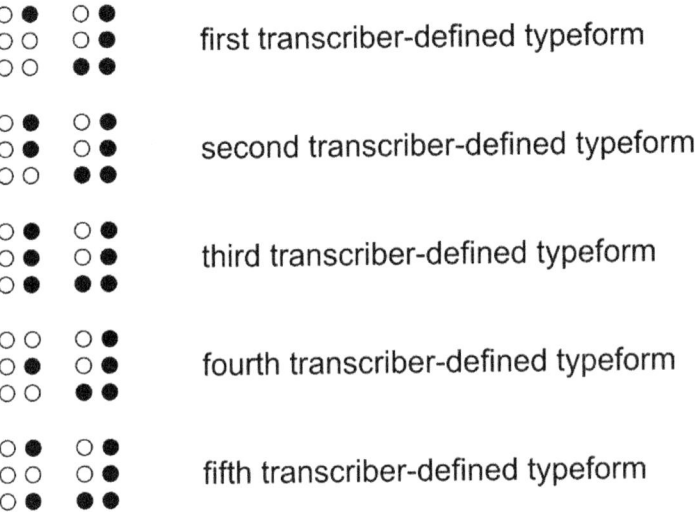

⠈⠀⠈⠨	first transcriber-defined typeform
⠈⠸⠀⠈⠨	second transcriber-defined typeform
⠈⠸⠈⠀⠈⠨⠀⠸	third transcriber-defined typeform
⠠⠀⠈⠨	fourth transcriber-defined typeform
⠈⠀⠈⠸⠀⠈⠨	fifth transcriber-defined typeform

Transcriber-defined typeforms are used to show a change in the font attribute such as font size if the meaning is beyond cosmetic. Transcriber-defined typeforms must be followed by a symbol indicator, word indicator, passage indicator or a terminator.

⠈⠀⠀⠈⠨⠀⠰⠰	first transcriber-defined typeform symbol indicator
⠈⠀⠀⠈⠨⠀⠰	first transcriber-defined typeform word indicator
⠈⠀⠀⠈⠨⠀⠀⠶⠶	first transcriber-defined typeform passage indicator
⠈⠀⠀⠈⠨⠀⠐	first transcriber-defined typeform terminator

Simple Arrows

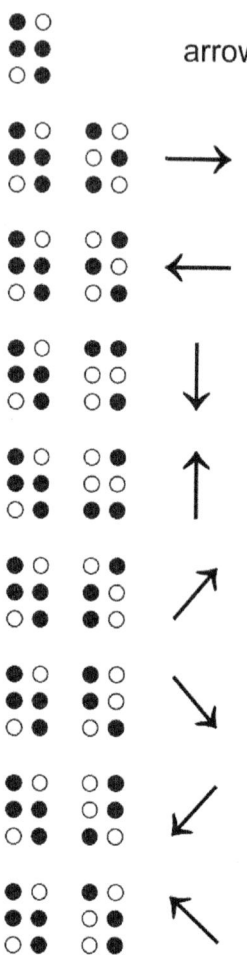

Use arrows as they would appear in printed text. The length and thickness of an arrow is not important.

Simple Shapes

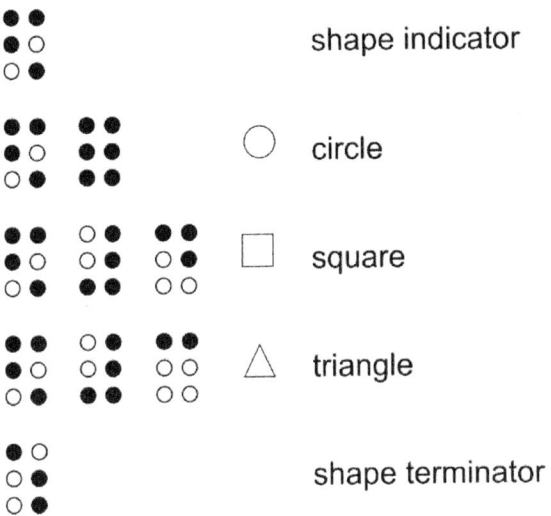

The braille sign for a square and equilateral triangle are based on the number of sides to their shape.

If a shape is followed by a space, the space will act as terminator.

```
   □            A  B  C  D
```

If a shape is next to a letter, punctuation or number – then a shape terminator is required.

```
   □            A  B  C  D
```

Transcriber-Defined Shapes

⠀⠨⠀⠀⠶⠀⠀⠀⠀⠀ transcriber-defined shape indicator

For complex shapes, a transcriber-defined shape indicator is used and this is followed by an appropriate word or set of initials.

A star shape could be defined as:

⠠⠀⠶⠀⠨⠀⠐⠀⠶⠀⠐
s t a r

A semi-circle shape could be defined as:

⠠⠀⠶⠀⠐⠀⠶
s c

Please note that all transcriber-defined shapes need to be described in either a transcriber's note or a Special Symbols Page.

UEB Music

♭ flat

♮ natural

♯ sharp

The music accidentals: flat, natural and sharp have recently been added to UEB (Unified English Braille). However, their use is limited to being in normal text.

the black key

between C and D is

C ♯

Please note that a hashtag looks similar to a sharp symbol in printed text but a hashtag is not slanted.

Transcribers and visually impaired musicians looking for information about braille music should refer to the *New International Manual of Braille Music Notation* which is the international standard agreed upon by the Braille Music Subcommittee of the World Blind Union and compiled by Bettye Krolick in 1996

Foreign Letters

Foreign letters include ligatures, accents and Greek letters.

Ligatured letters are letters that are conjoined, whilst accented letters have a small mark above or below a letter. Greek letters are often used in mathematics and science and the Greek alphabet has 24 letters:

Alpha
Beta
Gamma
Delta
Epsilon
Zeta
Eta
Theta
Iota
Kappa
Lamda
Mu
Nu
Xi
Omikron
Pi
Rho
Sigma
Tau
Upsilon
Phi
Chi
Psi
Omega

Ligatured Letters

ligature indicator

A ligature is when two letters are joined together. They are often found in foreign words such as læring and Old English spellings such as Æther.

The ligature indicator always goes between the ligatured letters.

l a   e r i n g

If the ligatured letters are in capitals, both letters must be brailled as capitals. Also, the ligature indicator does not terminate a capital letter.

A   E t h e r

Accented Letters

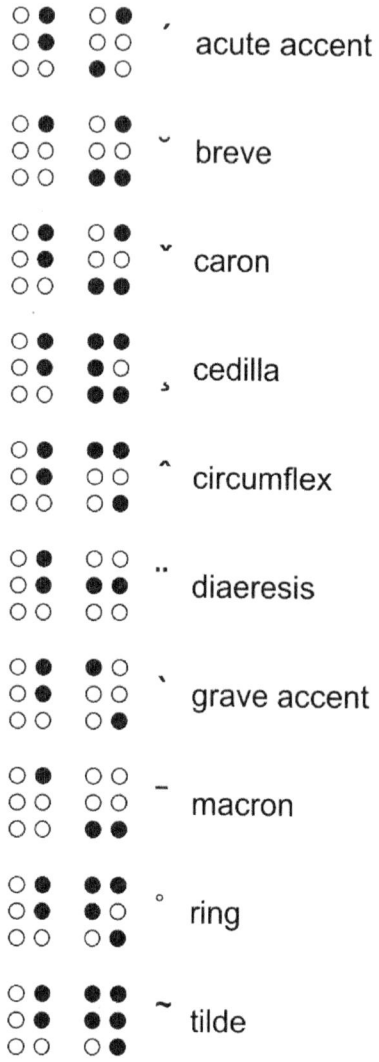

Place the braille sign for an accent before a letter.
Also, an accents would come after capital indicator.

Greek Letters

use ⠠ before each lowercase letter

⠁	⠃	⠛	⠙	⠑	⠵	⠱	⠹	⠊	⠅
α	β	γ	δ	ε	ζ	η	θ	ι	κ

⠇	⠍	⠝	⠭	⠕	⠏	⠗	⠎	⠞	⠥
λ	μ	ν	ξ	ο	π	ρ	σ	τ	υ

⠋	⠯	⠽	⠺
φ	χ	ψ	ω

use ⠈ ⠠ before each capital letter

⠁	⠃	⠛	⠙	⠑	⠵	⠱	⠹	⠊	⠅
Α	Β	Γ	Δ	Ε	Ζ	Η	Θ	Ι	Κ

⠇	⠍	⠝	⠭	⠕	⠏	⠗	⠎	⠞	⠥
Λ	Μ	Ν	Ξ	Ο	Π	Ρ	Σ	Τ	Υ

⠋	⠯	⠽	⠺
Φ	Χ	Ψ	Ω

Introduction to Contracted (Grade 2) Braille

Contracted braille was previously known as grade 2 braille. Most braille books are printed in contracted braille because they are less bulky and quicker to read.

The same letters, numbers and punctuation from uncontracted (grade 1) braille are still in use with contracted braille. However, contracted braille has the addition of a contraction system, which allows one or more braille cells to represent shorthand, common words and parts of words (usually prefixes and suffixes).

Since a braille cell can have a grade 1 and various grade 2 meanings, this book will also cover the rules that govern their usage.

Grade 1 Indicators

⠀⠐⠐   grade 1 symbol indicator

⠀⠐⠐ ⠀⠐⠐   grade 1 word indicator

⠀⠐⠐ ⠀⠐⠐ ⠀⠐⠐   grade 1 passage indicator

⠀⠐⠐ ⠀⠀⠠   grade 1 terminator

Most braille is written in grade 2 but a grade 1 indicator can be used to set grade 1 mode for a symbol, word or passage.

The grade 1 word indicator is terminated by either a space or a grade 1 terminator, whilst a grade 1 passage indicator can only be terminated by a grade 1 terminator.

Grade 1 indicators are used when a braille cell could be misread as any type of contraction. Grade 1 indicators are also used before words that are difficult to pronounce, foreign words and early forms of English such as those found in Shakespeare plays.

"O Romeo, Romeo! wherefore art thou Romeo?"

Alphabetic Wordsigns

An alphabetic wordsign is a single letter of the alphabet that represents a whole word.

Not every letter in the alphabet is used to create a wordsign. For instance, the letters a and i are not used because these letters are already words. Also, the alphabetic wordsign for the letter o used to represent the word o'clock but it has since been eliminated because of its awkwardness when it is brailled in capital letters.

The letters x and z are the only wordsigns that create words that do not begin with the same letter.

To use the alphabetic wordsigns properly, you will also need to learn these rules:

1) All alphabetic wordsigns must abide by the standing alone rule, which means that no letter, number or punctuation can be next to it
2) There is one exception to the standing alone rule for alphabetic wordsigns and that is an apostrophe, which can only be used if it is followed by any of these letters: d, ll, re, s, t, ve. This means that the word you'll would be brailled as y'll
3) Do not use an alphabetic wordsign to represent an acronym or abbreviation e.g. do not use the letter x for IT when its meaning is intended for Information Technology

Word	Wordsign
as	z
but	b
can	c
do	d
every	e
from	f
go	g
have	h
it	x
just	j
knowledge	k
like	l
more	m
not	n
people	p
quite	q
rather	r
so	s
that	t
us	u
very	v
will	w
you	y

Final-letter Groupsigns

Final-letter groupsigns are made up of two braille cells. The first braille cell is formed with either dots 56 or with dots 46 (see page 2). The second braille cell is the final letter of the part-word.

These are the rules that govern their use:

1) Final-letter groupsigns must be at the middle or end of a word e.g. **found**
2) A final-letter groupsign must follow a letter and it does not matter if the letters are accented, ligatured or if they form a contraction.
3) A final-letter groupsign cannot be used if it would follow a capital indicator, capital terminator, font attribute symbol or any type of punctuation (hyphens, apostrophes *etc*).
4) A final-letter groupsign cannot be used if it results in creating another word.
5) To prevent confusion, complex scientific words should not contain final-letter groupsigns
6) In the event of a word being separated between braille lines, do not use a final-letter groupsign if it would mean it would start at the beginning of a braille line.

The final-letter groupsigns **ness** and **ity** have additional rules to follow:

1) The final-letter group sign for **ness** cannot be used if a word ends with en or in and has a feminine meaning (e.g. citizeness)
2) It is important not to hinder pronunciation. Therefore, the final-letter groupsign for **ity** cannot be used for a word such as fruity.

Dots: 56

use ⠰ before groupsign

Part-word	Groupsign
ence	e
ong	g
ful	l
tion	n
ness	s
ment	t
ity	y

Dots: 46

use ⠘ before groupsign

Part-word	Groupsign
ound	d
ance	e
sion	n
less	s
ount	t

Initial-letter Contractions

Initial-letter contractions are made up of two braille cells. The first braille cell is formed with either dots 456, dot 5 or dots 45. The second braille cell is the first letter or letters of the word.

These are the general rules that govern their use:

1) All of the initial-letter contractions can be used as wordsigns or groupsigns i.e. as a whole word or as part of a word
2) Don't use initial-letter contractions if they have a serious effect on the pronunciation of a word e.g che**mother**apy can be difficult to interpret once it is brailled

Some initial-letter contractions have more specific rules that need to be followed and they will be discussed over the next few pages.

1) The initial-letter contraction for **had** must be pronounced with a 'short a'. For example, the word **had**dock is ok to use, but **Had**es is not ok to use. Some words such as **shad**ow are pronounced with a 'short a' but it cannot be used because strong groupsigns (such as sh) have preference over initial-letter contractions when the braille cells are of equal length

Dots: 456

use ⠸ before contraction

Word	Contraction
cannot	c
had	h
many	m
spirit	s
their	(the)
world	w

1) The letter e or the letter i cannot come before the initial-letter contraction **ever** e.g. beli**ever** is not allowed. Also, the first e in the word **ever** needs to be stressed i.e. the syllable would normally be spoken in a louder tone, a higher pitch or for a longer duration
2) **Here** is an initial-letter contraction that must be used when the word **here** is pronounced in one syllable e.g. atmosp**here** is ok to use, but do not use it in bot**here**d
3) **Name** is an initial-letter contraction that must be used when the word **name** is pronounced in one syllable e.g. sur**name** is ok to use, but not e**name**l
4) The initial-letter contraction for **one** must be used where it is pronounced as one syllable. However, an exception is made for the words honest and monetary as well as their derivitives e.g. honestly, dishonesty *etc*. Also, any words that end in oney can be used. Furthermore, it must be noted that the letter o cannot come before the initial-letter contraction for **one** e.g. no**one** is a word that cannot be used
5) The initial-letter contraction for **some** must be used where **some** is pronounced as one syllable within the basic word. This means that chromo**some** is ok to use but words such as ran**some**d cannot be used because although it is one syllable, the basic word for ransomed is ransom
6) The initial-letter contraction for **time** must be used in words that correctly pronounce the word time e.g. day**time** is ok to use, but not multi**time**dia

7) The letter a or the letter o cannot come before **under** e.g. la**under** is not allowed. Also, the letters un cannot create a prefix e.g. **under**ived is not allowed, but pl**under** is ok

Dot: 5

use ⠈ before contraction

Word	Contraction
character	(ch)
day	d
ever	e
father	f
here	h
know	k
lord	l
mother	m
name	n
one	o
ought	(ou)
part	p
question	q
right	r
some	s
there	(the)
time	t
through	(th)
under	u
where	(wh)
work	w
young	y

1) The initial-letter contractions: **there, these, those, upon** and **whose** must keep their meaning. For example, here**upon** is ok to use, but co**upon** cannot be used.

Dots: 45

use ⠐⠐ before contraction

Word	Contraction
these	(the)
those	(th)
upon	u
whose	(wh)
word	w

Strong Wordsigns

Strong wordsigns have braille cells with dots on the upper and lower rows as well as on the left and right columns. They can only form whole words.

These are the rules that govern their use:

1) The strong wordsigns: **child**, **out**, **shall**, **still**, **this** and **which** must be standing alone
2) An apostrophe can follow a strong wordsign but it must be followed by one of these letters: d, ll, re, s, t, ve

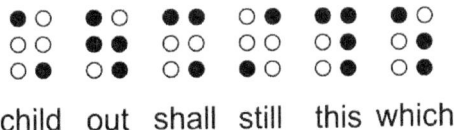

Strong Groupsigns

Strong groupsigns have braille cells with dots on the upper and lower rows as well as on the left and right columns. They can only be used to form part of a word.

These are the rules that govern their use:

1) Use the strong groupsigns: **ch**, **ou**, **sh**, **st**, **th** and **wh** if they will not be misread as the strong wordsigns: child, out, shall, still, this and which
2) Do not use the strong groupsigns: **ch**, **gh**, **sh**, **th** or **wh** if there is an aspirated 'h' e.g shape is ok to use, but mishap is not ok to use
3) The strong groupsign **ing** cannot be used at the beginning of a word, it must follow a space, hyphen or dash e.g. finger is ok to use, but ingot is not ok use to
4) If a letter is accented or ligatured, do not use a strong groupsign (or any other type of contraction for that matter)
5) Pronunciation is important so do not use strong groupsigns to bridge compound words such as sweetheart

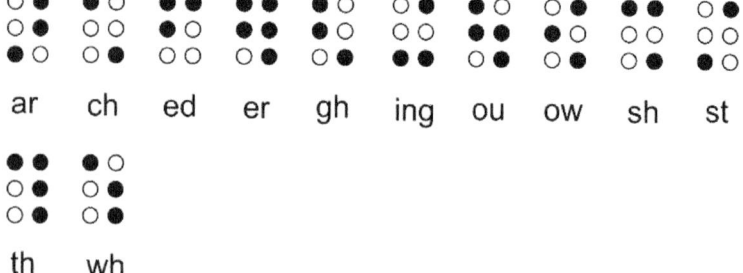

Strong Contractions

Strong contractions have braille cells with dots on the upper and lower rows as well as on the left and right columns. They can be used to form a whole word or part of a word.

These are the rules that govern their use:

1) Strong contractions are very common in usage and have preference over every other type of wordsign, groupsign and contraction, unless fewer braille cells can be used to spell a word e.g. the word 'thence' would use 4 cells with a strong contraction, but only 3 cells with a strong groupsign **th** followed by a final-letter groupsign **ence**
2) A strong contraction should not be used if it impacts the pronunciation e.g. do not use in the word sweetheart

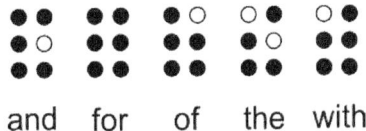

and   for   of   the   with

Lower Groupsigns

Lower groupsigns have no upper dots (dot 1 or dot 4) and form part of a word. They must abide by the Lower Sign Rule, which means that lower groupsigns can be used with letters, contractions and punctuation, as long as there is a sign with an upper dot somewhere within a sequence of any number of characters and spaces. Quotation marks are not counted as having upper dots for this rule.

Specific rules for lower groupsigns that can only be used at the beginning of a word:

1) The lower groupsigns **be**, **con** and **dis** must be at the beginning of a word and form the first syllable e.g. behave is ok to use, but betting is not ok.
2) A hyphen or dash can come before **be**, **con** and **dis** as long as it forms the first syllable of a word e.g. self-confidence
3) The indicator and terminator symbol for capital and font attributes must not come after **be**, **con** or **dis** e.g. concern is ok to use but con<u>cern</u> is not ok to use
4) Punctuation such as brackets, apostrophes and quotation marks must not come after **be**, **con** or **dis** e.g. "believe" is ok but dis(like) is not ok to use
5) Common abbreviations with at least one other letter are allowed e.g. cont (continued)

Specific rules for lower groupsigns that can only be used at the middle of a word:

1) The lower groupsigns **ea, bb, cc, ff** and **gg** must be at the middle of a word e.g. piggy
2) A hyphen or an apostrophe cannot be used before or after **ea, bb, cc, ff** or **gg** e.g. cliff-top cannot be used
3) A capital indicator or capital terminator must not come before or after **ea, bb, cc, ff** or **gg** e.g. SeaWorld cannot be used
4) Do not use **ea** if it forms a prefix e.g. reactive cannot be used

Specific rules for lower groupsigns that can be used at any part of a word:

1) The lower groupsigns **en** and **in** can be used at the beginning, middle or end of a word e.g. en<u>d</u>

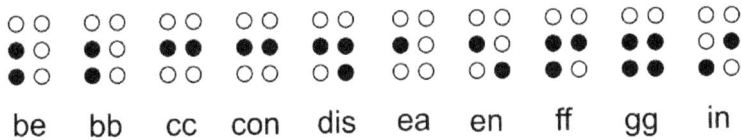

Lower Wordsigns

Lower wordsigns have no upper dots (dot 1 or dot 4) and can only form whole words. They must abide by the Lower Sign Rule and the Standing Alone Rule, which means that there must be a space, hyphen or dash that is before or after the lower wordsign. Indicators, terminators and punctuation can be used.

These are the specific rules that apply to the lower wordsigns:

1) The lower wordsigns for **be**, **his**, **was** and **were** have the same braille cells as punctuation symbols (semi-colon, opening quotation mark, closing quotation mark and round brackets). Therefore, these lower wordsigns must not be next to any type of punctuation with only lower dots, including hyphens and dashes.
2) The lower wordsigns for **in** and **enough** must be part of a sequence that has at least one cell with an upper dot. The only exception to this, is if there is a capital indicator or capital terminator in the sequence.
3) An apostrophe can only be used in the lower wordsign **enough** e.g enough's

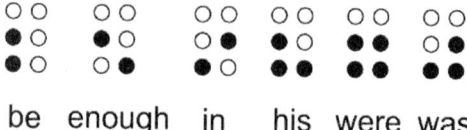

Shortforms

A shortform is a shortened form of a word. This means that only some of the letters of a word are brailled (e.g. the word **about** is brailled with the letters **ab**)

There is a total of 75 shortforms to remember, which may seem like a lot at first but it will soon become second nature. You may notice that words such as **much** has the shortform **m(ch)**. The brackets are not brailled but the letters in these brackets represent a contraction which does need to be brailled.

Once you have committed the shortforms to memory, you will need to remember the following rules:

1) Shortforms can be used to represent a word that is standing alone, with or without an apostrophe e.g. friend's
2) Shortforms can be used for a whole person's name such as Mr **Little** but not for part of a name such as Mr **Good**win
3) Either a space, hyphen or dash must come before and after shortforms that form part of a word e.g. **good**-bye
4) The meaning and pronunciation does not need to be kept when using shortforms to form part of a word e.g. (should)er
5) Shortforms that begin with **be** or **con** must be at the beginning of part of a word. For example, do not use mis**conceive**

6) The following shortforms: **blind, first, friend, good, letter, little** and **quick** must be a whole word or form the beginning of part of a word. Furthermore, they cannot be followed by either a vowel or the letter y when used to create part of a word. For example, do not use a shortform in words such as **blind**ing
7) The shortforms: **children** and **after** can be whole words or form part of a word but they must not be followed by a vowel or the letter y. For example God**children**
8) Capital, font or transcriber indicators must only be used at the beginning of a word. Their terminator indicators must be used at the end of a word.
9) Shortforms must not be part of a word that contains any numbers or symbols e.g. forward backward slashes, asterisks *etc*
10) Punctuation must be in its grammatically correct place. This means that quotation marks, brackets and full stops must be at the end of a word. For this reason, shortforms cannot be used for email or web addresses due to a fullstop being used in the middle of a word.
11) The letters forming a shortform must not be separated between the braille lines. Also, a hyphen should be added to show that it is still one word e.g.

                                                friend-
liness

Word	Shortform	Word	Shortform
about	ab	herself	h(er)f
above	abv	him	hm
according	ac	himself	hmf
across	acr	immediate	imm
after	af	its	xs
afternoon	afn	itself	xf
afterward	afw	letter	lr
again	ag	little	ll
against	ag(st)	much	m(ch)
almost	alm	must	m(st)
already	alr	myself	myf
also	al	necessary	nec
although	al(th)	neither	nei
altogether	alt	oneself	(one)f
always	alw	ourselves	(ou)rvs
because	bc	paid	pd
before	bf	perceive	p(er)cv
behind	bh	perceiving	p(er)cvg
below	bl	perhaps	p(er)h
beneath	bn	quick	qk
beside	bs	receive	rcv
between	bt	receiving	rcvg
beyond	by	rejoice	rjc
blind	bl	rejoicing	rjcg
braille	brl	said	sd
children	(ch)n	should	(sh)d
conceive	(con)cv	such	s(ch)
conceiving	(con)cvg	themselves	(the)mvs
could	cd	thyself	(th)yf
deceive	dcv	today	td
deceiving	dcvg	together	tgr
declare	dcl	tomorrow	tm
declaring	dclg	tonight	tn
either	ei	would	wd
first	f(st)	your	yr
friend	fr	yourself	yrf
good	gd	yourselves	yrvs
great	grt		

Preferences

Some words can be brailled in multiple ways by using different contractions. It is therefore important to give preference to one way over another.

The highest preference is given to the contraction that saves the most space, unless it's pronunciation is seriously affected.

If the number of braille cells occupies the same amount of space, then this is the order of preference:

1) Wordsigns and shortforms
2) Strong contractions
3) Strong groupsigns
4) Lower groupsigns
5) Initial-letter contractions and final-letter groupsigns

Please note that the lower groupsigns: **be**, **con** and **dis** can have preference over strong groupsigns when be, con or dis form the first syllable of a word e.g. distance

Braille Courses

To gain a certification in Unified English Braille, simply complete a course that best matches your needs:

Hadley Institute for the Blind and Visually Impaired
http://www.hadley.edu/FindaCourse.asp

National Federation of the Blind
https://nfb.org/braille-transcribing

RNIB (Royal National Institute for the Blind)
http://www.rnib.org.uk/braille-and-moon-%E2%80%93-tactile-codes-learning-braille/braille-courses-adults

UEBOnline - Braille training for sighted learners
http://uebonline.org/

UEBOT (Unified English Braille Online Training)
http://uebot.niu.edu/

Bibliography

Braille Authority of North America (2014) The ABCs of UEB: A Guide for the Transition from English Braille American Edition (EBAE) to The Rules of Unified English Braille (UEB). Available at: http://www.brailleauthority.org/ueb/abcs/abcs-ueb.html

Braille Authority of North America (n.d.) Braille Symbols and Indicators. [pdf] Available at: http://www.brailleauthority.org/ueb/symbols_list.pdf

Braille Authority of North America (n.d.) Braille Basics. [pdf] Available at: http://www.brailleauthority.org/learn/braillebasic.pdf

ClearVision children's braille library and Linden Lodge School (2013) Unified English Braille: What's it all about? [pdf] Available at: http://www.clearvisionproject.org/ueb.pdf

Dover Christ Church Academy, (n.d.), Literacy: Punctuation revision and worksheets. [pdf] Available at: http://www.dccacademy.org.uk/parents_information/downloads/Literacy_punctuation_pack_for_Parents.pdf

Duxbury Systems (2008) UEB Braille Chart. [pdf] Available at: http://duxburysystems.com/images/ueb_black.pdf

Grammar Monster, (n.d.) Punctuation. Available at: http://www.grammar-monster.com/

Jane Straus (2008) The Blue Book of Grammar and Punctuation: Tenth Edition. [pdf] Available at: http://www.ereading.club/bookreader.php/134334/The_Blue_Book_of_Grammar_and_Punctuation.pdf

Jordan Penn, (n.d.) The Punctuation Guide. Available at: http://www.thepunctuationguide.com/brackets.html

Round Table on Information Access for People with Print Disabilities Inc and International Council on English Braille (2013) The Rules of English Unified Braile: Second Edition 2013. [pdf] Available at: http://www.iceb.org/Rules%20of%20Unified%20English%20Braille%202013%20(linked).pdf

Round Table on Information Access for People with Print Disabilities Inc. and Australian Braille Authority (2014) Unified English Braille: Australian Training Manual, Revised April 2014. [pdf] Available at: http://brailleaustralia.org/wp-content/uploads/2013/10/UEB-Australian-Training-Manual-Revised-April-2014.pdf

UK Association for Accessible Formats (December 2012) Unified English Braille (UEB): Summary of changes for ordinary braille [pdf]. Available at: http://www.ukaaf.org/wp-content/uploads/2015/05/UEB-Summary-pdf.pdf

Wisconsin Center for the Blind and Visually Impaired (n.d.) Introduction to Unified Braille. Available at: http://www.wcbvi.k12.wi.us/outreach/professional-development/ueb-introduction/

Printed in Great Britain
by Amazon